CRISPY on the OUTSIDE

FRESH & WARM on the inside

this is the MAGIC OF PIES

the EASIEST PIE MAKER BOOK ever!

4 Ingredients
PO Box 400
Caloundra QLD 4551
+61 431 297 923
ABN: 17 435 679 521

🌐 4ingredients.com.au
📘 facebook.com/4ingredientspage
▶️ 4 ingredients Channel
🐦 @4ingredients
📌 @4ingredients
📷 4 Ingredients
✉️ info@4ingredients.com.au

Photography & Stylists:	Kim McCosker, Melinda Dines, Leonie Wohlsen
Design & Formatting:	Shem Hunter www.shemhunter.com
Publisher:	4 Ingredients
Distribution:	Simon & Schuster, Australia
	Simon & Schuster, New Zealand
ISBN:	978-0-6484851-7-9

the EASIEST PIE MAKER BOOK *ever!*

Like me, you've bought a Pie Maker, in fact, you may own a couple because you have fallen truly, madly, deeply in love with them ♡. Honestly, it has become one of my favourite appliances EVER! Whether you are making sweet or savoury pies, pies with pastry or without, beef, chicken or vegetarian pies, pikelets, crumpets or cupcakes, a pie maker can do it all!

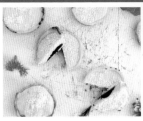

YOU WILL NOT BELIEVE WHAT YOU CAN MAKE IN YOUR PIE MAKER!

To me, pies represent a little **parcel of thoughtfulness.** Traditionally, pies were made of a simple flour and water paste wrapped around meat, which helped cook the meat and lock in its juices, back in a time when nothing was wasted. Today the practice continues, as there is nothing simpler than using leftovers to create a delicious pie for lunch the next day or stewing plentiful, seasonal fruits to fill their warm, snug interiors.

Quick, easy and delicious... Long may the humble pie bring us together with **comfort and love.**

Kim

Guide to Weights & Measures

To help a recipe turn out right, you need to measure right.
I have included this simple conversion table to help, regardless of where you are in the world.

Grams – pounds & ounces

Grams (g)	Ounces (oz.)	Grams (g)	Ounces (oz.)
5 g	¼ oz.	225 g	9 oz.
10 g	½ oz.	250 g	10 oz.
25 g	1 oz.	275 g	11 oz.
50 g	2 oz.	300 g	12 oz.
75 g	3 oz.	325 g	13 oz.
100 g	4 oz.	350 g	14 oz.
125 g	5 oz.	375 g	15 oz.
150 g	6 oz.	400 g	1 pound (lb.)
175 g	7 oz.	700 g	1½ lb.
200 g	8 oz.	900 g	2 lb.

Spoons – millilitres (ml)

1 teaspoon	5 ml
1 dessertspoon	10 ml
1 tablespoon	15 ml

Cups – ml – fluid ounces – tablespoons

Cups	ml	Fluid Ounces	Tbsp.
⅛ cup	30 ml	1 fl oz.	2
¼ cup	60 ml	2 fl oz.	4
⅓ cup	80 ml	2.5 fl oz.	5.5
½ cup	125 ml	4 fl oz.	8
⅔ cup	160 ml	5 fl oz.	10.5
¾ cup	190 ml	6 fl oz.	12
1 cup	250 ml	8 fl oz.	16

Contents

The History of Pies

YES ... We have the Egyptians to thank for many things – Pies being one of them. Pies started to be baked by the Egyptians in 9500BC.

The Egyptians made 'galettes', honey-filled treats similar to pies but baked over hot coals. They became known to the Romans through the Greeks. Thereafter, the Romans made pies known to the rest of Europe and eventually, the world.

Originally, pies were baked in wood-fired ovens (can you image today's delicate puff pastry in those?) Back then, the crust was both a pan and a lid, and was used to protect the meat that was cooking inside. It was tricky to make kitchenware that could withstand the heat of the oven without exploding or deforming. Thick dough was the ideal shell to protect the food from the fire and allow an even cook. For a long time, the crust was supposedly not eaten. Dried up and often burnt, thick, unleavened and hard, back then the chooks probably didn't even eat it!

Thankfully, with experience, the Romans learnt better cooking techniques, placing the pies into the oven earlier before the heat was so intense. Cooking them at the opening where the heat is less, circulating them, cooking more or less at once. Practices that over time improved and helped them create a delicious pie, all of which could be eaten and enjoyed by many.

Fast forward to today, there is quite the geographical variation to what a pie is in the world.

- **America:** Pies are mostly sweet and deep, they can have a top crust but always have a bottom crust (think Pumpkin Pie, Cherry Pie & everyone's fave Apple Pie).

- **Great Britain & Germany:** Pies are mostly savoury and are fully enclosed in crusts, base, sides and top (think Pork Pies).

- **Sweden:** Pies are still savoury, but shallow and open-faced, similar to France and Italy (often sweet and better known as 'Tarts').

- **Australia:** Where we love them all. In fact, Australian's eat on average 12 meat pies each, every single year. That's a whopping 270 million meat pies a year.

- **New Zealand:** Think that's impressive? Our 'cussies' across 'the ditch' eat on average 15 meat pies each, every single year. That's 66 million meat pies every single year!

What is apparent, is that for a very long time, throughout the world, people everywhere have enjoyed pies. I have a feeling this will continue well into the future.

LONG LIVE THE HUMBLE PIE!

[1] https://www.foodstandards.gov.au/consumer/generalissues/meatpie/Pages/default.aspx

Tips 4 Incredible Pie Making

I own two different Pie Makers. As a mum of 3 teenage boys, I often find myself using the larger ¾ cup 4-hole Sunbeam Pie Magic for savoury pies and the smaller K-Mart ⅓ cup 4-hole Pie Maker for sweet pies. Only you know who you are cooking for, how many people, their ages and appetites, so regardless of the machine you have, just adapt the recipes within to the amount of filling you need to satisfy your family. Here follows a list of useful tips that were shared on the 4 Ingredients Facebook page when I first announced I would be writing The Easiest Pie Maker Book Ever.

1. When first using your Pie Maker, heat for 5 minutes, brush lightly with oil and allow to cool. This is called 'seasoning' and once done, nothing will ever stick again.

2. When making multiple batches of pies wipe the pie holes clean with damp paper towel after each batch.

3. Freeze grated cheese to stop it going mouldy.

4. Most meat fillings can be made ahead and refrigerated. They also freeze well.

5. When making savoury pies, I often use shortcrust on the bottom and puff on the top.

6. To make *POACHED EGG:* Simply crack 4 eggs into each pie hole. Close lid and cook for 4 minutes for a runny centre. 6 minutes for a hard centre.

7. *Pie Maker FRY-UP:* Thank you Belinda Foreman for this. Eggs in two pie holes, chopped mushies in one and chopped chorizo and onion in the other. Cook for 5 minutes. Serve on toast or with a bed of fresh baby spinach.

8. *TO CLEAN:* Dampen 2 paper towels, lay across the top of the Pie Maker (overlapping is fine). Close lid and cook for 4 minutes for a good steam-clean.

9. Thank you Amanda Smith for sharing this image on the 4 Ingredients Facebook Page. We are unsure of its origin but would like to say 'THANK YOU'. I don't know why I hadn't thought of it before. Simply place 4 sheets of puff pastry together to cut 9 large bases from them.

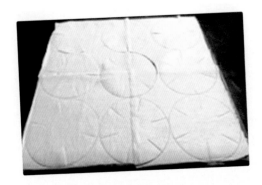

Q: I've been having problems with my tops not cooking properly, they sink in and don't cook evenly, anyone else?

A: Make sure you put enough filling into each pie so when you put your pastry top on, it reaches the concave surface of the top plate and browns beautifully.

Q: Does anyone do anything with leftover Silverside in their Pie Makers?

A: I cook my silverside in chicken noodle soup, add enough water to cover silverside then add 2 packets of soup. When ready, thicken the soup with a cornflour paste. Shred any leftovers, add mixed veggies and sauce and make yummy pies.

Q: I'd like to know if I can blind bake just the pie crust in the maker without the filling?

A: Yes, I do. Just put your pastry in as normal then a piece of baking paper and fill with raw rice and cook for 2 or 3 minutes.

Q: Can anyone tell me how to make an easy custard tart?

A: *CUSTARD TARTS / MAKES 8*
Whip up 1 pkt Cottees Vanilla Dessert, 300ml cream and 150ml milk.
Refrigerate 30 minutes. Remove. Stir. Cut 8 bases from 2 sheets puff pastry.
Place into Pie Maker holes. Fill with custard. Bake 6 minutes.

Tips 4 Glorious Gluten Free Pie Crusts

Writing this book, I predominantly used store-bought pastry, breads and wraps for the pies. These days, gluten free variations are readily available. However, if you prefer to make your own, here's a couple of my favourites.

Gluten Free Pie Crust

- 8 tbsp. butter, room temperature
- 100g cream cheese, room temperature
- ¼ cup thickened cream

- 1½ cups gluten free plain flour
  (I used Well & Good's gluten free pastry flour)
- ½ tsp. coarse salt

Using hand-held beaters, cream the butter, cream cheese and cream to thoroughly combine. Add the flour and salt and blend until smooth. Wrap the dough in cling wrap and refrigerate for 2 hours. The dough will be very firm, take a rolling pin and pound the dough using a dusting of gluten free flour on a clean surface, until it is soft enough to roll out. As it will be a little crumbly, roll the dough on baking paper.

NB: I have found, homemade gluten free pastry works best as one large pie round. Make it as thick as you can in the pie dish, it will hold together better.

Easy Sweet Pastry

- 1¾ cups gluten free plain flour
- ½ cup icing sugar
- 125g cold butter, cut into cubes
- 125g soft cream cheese
- 1 egg yolk

Put flour and icing sugar into a food processor and pulse until combined. With the motor running add the cold butter, followed by the cream cheese. Add the egg yolk and mix until dough forms a ball. Remove dough and wrap in cling wrap, refrigerate for 15 minutes. On a clean, dry surface, roll into a 2mm thickness and use to make sweet tarts and pastries. Can be sealed in an airtight container for up to 3 or 4 days.

Store-bought gluten free pastry

- Allow store-bought gluten free pastry to defrost for 15 minutes before using.
- Store-bought gluten free pastry looks thin and nice enough to use. But it works so much better if you roll it out a little further.

Homemade gluten free pastry

- The way puff pastry is made is by rubbing butter into flour. This leaves big pieces of butter in the flour so that when it cooks, the butter creates pockets of air; resulting in flaky pastry.
- When making pastry at home, every time you squish it together and re-roll it out, you are actually breaking down the butter which will result in a less flaky pastry.

BREAKFAST PIES

Bacon & Egg Quiches
Makes 4

- 6 slices bacon, cut in half lengthways
- 6 eggs
- 2 tbsp. grated Parmesan cheese
- 2 tbsp. chopped shallots

Preheat Pie Maker.

Line each pie hole with bacon, one half one way, the other half the other.

Into each, crack an egg.

Season with sea salt and cracked pepper and sprinkle with Parmesan and half the shallots.

Cover and cook for 4 to 5 minutes for a slightly runny egg, 6 minutes for a soft-boiled egg, or 8 minutes for a hard-boiled egg.

Zucchini Breakfast Quiches

Gently squeeze excess liquid from 1 grated zucchini. In a bowl whisk 4 eggs until light and fluffy. Season well, then add ½ cup grated cheddar cheese, stir to combine. Line each pie hole with bacon. Fill each pie hole with mixture. Sprinkle with a little more cheese and season. Close lid and cook for 8 minutes.

Breakfast Pies
Makes 4 Large

- 4 shortcut slices bacon, chopped
- 2 shallots, chopped
- 4 eggs
- 4 slices buttered bread, crusts removed

In a frying pan over medium heat, sauté bacon, stirring for 2 minutes.

Add shallots and cook for 2 minutes, stirring often.

Press the bread slices into each pie hole.

Sprinkle with bacon and shallot.

Crack an egg into each, sprinkle with a little more shallot and bacon and season.

Close the lid and cook for 8 minutes, or until the crust is gold and the egg cooked.

VARIATION

Line 4 pie holes with puff pastry.

Crack an egg into each.

Sprinkle with grated cheese, diced mushroom and bacon.

Season. Close lid. Cook for 8 minutes.

Condensed Milk French Toast
Makes 8

In France, French Toast is called 'pain perdu,' meaning 'lost bread'.
Why lost bread? Because this is the perfect use for stale or 'lost bread'.

- **4 eggs**
- **½ cup condensed milk**
- **6 slices raisin loaf, quartered**
- **¼ cup maple syrup**

Preheat Pie Maker.

In a bowl, whisk eggs.

Add condensed milk and stir to combine.

In batches, soak each quarter of raisin loaf
for two minutes, flipping halfway through.

Layer 3 slices into each pie hole.

Close lid and cook for 4 minutes.

Carefully remove and repeat.

*OPTIONAL: Serve each drizzled with maple syrup
and with a scoop of creamy ice-cream.*

Condensed Milk Pancakes
Makes 8 Large

- 1 cup self-raising flour
- 1 egg
- ¼ can condensed milk (around 100g)
- ¾ cup milk

In a bowl place the flour and make a well.

Add remaining ingredients and season with salt.

Using a fork, whisk until combined.

Rest for 15 minutes.

Heat Pie Maker.

Lightly grease each pie hole, add ¼ cup mixture to each pie hole.

Close lid, cook 3 minutes, flip and cook for another 3 minutes.

Using a fork, gently remove.

Repeat.

OPTIONAL: Use 1 cup of milk instead of condensed milk. Just flavour the mixture with orange zest or ground cinnamon before cooking.

KEEP CALM AND EAT PANCAKES

Crumpets

Makes 8

Crumpets are a treat known throughout the Commonwealth. Of Anglo-Saxon origin, they have been around since the 1300s, and served warm spread with butter and golden syrup, chances are they will be around for another 1300 years.

- 2 cups plain flour
- 1 tbsp. baking powder
- ¾ tsp. sugar
- ¾ tsp. sea salt

- 1 tsp. dried yeast
- 1½ cups lukewarm water

Sift flour, baking powder, sugar, salt and yeast into a bowl.

Add the water and mix to combine, until nice and smooth.

Preheat Pie Maker.

Fill each round with ¼ cup batter.

Cook for about 8 minutes with lid up.

Turn over and cook for 1 minute to lightly brown the top.

Easy Berry Pancakes
Makes 8

This recipe is courtesy of Sunbeam Australia who created it for their Sunbeam Pie Magic® Maker. I loved the simplicity of it the very SECOND I saw it and have made it with several variations; blueberries, blackberries, strawberries and bananas.

- **1 pancake mix bottle**
- **125g fresh raspberries**

Follow pancake bottle instructions.

Pour ¼ cup batter into each Sunbeam Pie Magic® dish, adding 5 raspberries on each.

Cover raspberries with 1 tablespoon of batter.

Close lid, turn on and cook for 8 minutes.

Carefully flip over and cook for a further 4 minutes.

Repeat processes with remaining batter.

OPTIONAL: Serve with maple syrup and fresh raspberries.

Eggs 'n' Peppers
Makes 4

We often say 'If you have eggs, you have a meal!'
They are such a versatile ingredient and pair well with so many things.

- 1 red capsicum
- 4 eggs
- 1 tbsp. sweet chilli jam
- 8 fresh basil leaves

Rinse the capsicum, remove the stem and seeds and cut 4 big rings from it.

Place each ring into the pie holes of a large Pie Maker (if using a small Pie Maker you may need to break the ring and wrap it around itself).

Into each, crack an egg.

Drizzle with sweet chilli jam and fresh basil leaves.

Close lid and cook, 6 minutes for a soft-boiled egg, 8 minutes for a hard-boiled egg.

Remove, season and serve.

Baked Eggs in Tomatoes

Use a small, round tomato, scoop out most of its interior, removing the core and seeds, season with sea salt, cracked pepper and fresh thyme. Crack an egg into it and cook for 8 minutes. Serve with a little Parmesan cheese and more fresh thyme.

Hash Brown Breakfast Pies

Makes 4

- 2 large waxy potatoes, peeled
- 4 eggs, seasoned and whisked
- ½ cup grated cheddar cheese
- 2 slices bacon, chopped

Peel and grate the potatoes.

Squeeze out excess liquid and season.

Lightly oil the holes of the Pie Maker.

Separate the grated potato into quarters and press each quarter into the base and up the sides of the pie hole making a nest.

Cook for 5 minutes or until just starting to brown.

Divide egg mixture evenly across each nest.

Top with grated cheese and chopped bacon.

Season.

Cook for 7 minutes or until golden.

who cares about
HASH TAGS
when there's
HASH BROWNS

Mini-Toad-In-The-Hole
Makes 4 Large / 6 Small

'Toad-in-the-hole' first appeared in print in 1762. No one knows for sure how this dish received its name, but there is much speculation. The most common and accepted story is that the sight of bangers (sausages) poking through the rich batter resembled frogs peering out of a crevice in the ground... 'Toad-in-the-hole!'

- 6 chipolatas
- 1 tbsp. butter, melted
- 2 eggs
- ½ cup milk

- ½ cup self-raising flour

Brown the chipolatas in a non-stick frying pan over medium high heat, turning often to cook through.

Lightly oil the holes of the Pie Maker.

In a bowl whisk eggs constantly for 3 to 4 minutes or until light and fluffy.

Gradually add milk, whisking constantly.

Season generously with sea salt and cracked pepper (½ tsp. each) and add the flour, gently whisking to combine.

Cut the chipolatas in half diagonally and place two halves into each pie hole.

Pour ¼ cup of the batter over each.

Close lid and cook for 8 minutes.

Remove and repeat with remaining ingredients.

OPTIONAL: Serve with ketchup or tomato sauce.

Sunny-Side Up Eggs

Makes 4

- 4 slices bread
- 4 eggs
- 4 tbsp. BBQ Sauce
- 2 tbsp. freshly chopped parsley

Spread butter across one side of
each slice of bread, and BBQ sauce
on the other.

Press the bread, butter side down,
into each pie hole.

Crack an egg into each and season
with fresh parsley and cracked pepper.

Close the lid and cook for 8 minutes,
or until the crust is gold and the egg cooked.

turn your
face
towards the
sun
and the shadows
fall behind you

Omelettes
Makes 4 Large / 6 Small

- 4 eggs
- 1 shallot, finely chopped
  (reserve a little for garnish)
- ⅓ cup finely diced bacon

- 2 tbsp. grated mozzarella cheese
- 3 cherry tomatoes

In a bowl, whisk the eggs.

Add the shallot, cooked bacon and Mozzarella, season with sea salt and cracked pepper and stir to combine.

Pour enough mixture to come just to the top of the pie holes.

Top with a half a cherry tomato.

Close and cook for 7 minutes or until cooked through.

Transfer to a plate and repeat with the remaining mixture.

Serve scattered with extra shallot.

OPTIONAL: Serve with a splash of Sweet Chilli Jam.

you can't make an
omelette
without breaking a few
eggs

LUNCH
PIES

Asparagus Mornay Savoury Cases
Makes 6 Large

- 3 tbsp. unsalted butter
- 3 tbsp. plain flour
- 1½ cups milk
- 415g can asparagus spears (or cuts), drained
- ½ cup grated cheddar cheese
- 1 tbsp. lemon zest
- 6 slices wholegrain bread, crusts removed

Into a saucepan over a medium heat, melt the butter.

Add flour and stir to incorporate.

Reduce heat and gradually add the milk, stirring constantly.

Season well. Increase heat and bring to a gentle boil.

Add the drained asparagus, cheddar cheese and lemon.

Stir until well combined; reduce heat and simmer 5 minutes.

Lightly butter one side of each slice of bread.

Place the buttered side down into each hole.

Close and cook for 4 minutes.

Add asparagus filling, almost level and cook for another 4 minutes.

Remove and serve with your favourite salad.

Curried Prawn Savoury Cases

Do the same as above, make the white sauce. Add 1 tsp. curry powder and 12 green prawns, peeled and chopped. Stir to combine. Reduce heat and simmer. Cook as above. ENJOY!

Carbonara Cups
Makes 8 Large

So originally, we were discussing suitable filling combinations for mushrooms when we thought about this one. Tried both in mushrooms and in bread cases, both equally delicious. Mushrooms however, would make this dish Gluten Free.

- 200g bacon, finely diced
- 250g cream cheese
- ¼ cup shallots, finely chopped
- ¾ cup fresh grated Parmesan cheese
- 8 slices bread, crusts
- 1 tbsp. butter

In a non-stick frying pan, sauté bacon until nice and golden.

Drain and cool slightly.

In a bowl, mix cream cheese, shallots, bacon and Parmesan together; season with cracked pepper.

Butter one side of each slice of bread.

Press the buttered side down into each hole.

Close lid and cook 4 minutes.

Fill each ¾ full with mixture.

Close lid and cook for 4 minutes.

Carefully remove and repeat.

Cheeseburger Pies

Makes 8 Large / 12 Small

We made many a marvellous discovery when writing this cookbook, but this pie rates as one of the best. Truly a delicious pie!

- 1 onion, finely chopped
- 500g minced beef
- 1 tbsp. plain flour
- 1 tbsp. beef stock powder
- ⅓ cup BBQ sauce

- 1 tbsp. mustard
- 3 sheets puff pastry
- 80g cheddar cheese, thinly sliced
- ½ cup sliced pickles

Sauté onions in a non-stick frying pan over a medium heat until just soft, 4 minutes.

Add mince, using a fork, break up and cook stirring until browned, 6 minutes.

Into 1 cup of water, mix the flour and stock and stir.

Reduce heat, add the liquid and stir continuously until nice and thick.

Add BBQ sauce and mustard and stir well until sauce has thickened.

Season to taste.

Meanwhile, lay the 3 sheets of puff pastry side by side (slightly overlapping).

Using a rolling pin, roll to connect.

Cut 8 bases and lids from the sheets.

Place 4 bases of pastry into Pie Maker, fill with meat and a layer of cheddar cheese and pickles.

Cover with pastry lids.

Close the machine and cook for 10 minutes.

Carefully remove and repeat.

Chicken, Leek & Mushroom Pies
Makes 6 Small

- 2 chicken breast fillets, chopped into small 1cm pieces
- 1 leek
- 2 cloves garlic
- 2 tbsp. butter
- 150g mushrooms, sliced
- ¾ cup cream
- 2 sheets puff pastry

Thinly slice the leek and crush the garlic.

In a non-stick frying pan over medium heat, melt the butter.

Sauté the leek and garlic until soft and tender.

Add chopped chicken, cook for 4 minutes, tossing to cook evenly.

Add mushroom, season and cook, 3 minutes.

Reduce heat and add cream, simmer for 20 minutes.

Meanwhile cut 6 small bases and lids from the pastry.

Press the first 4 bases into each hole.

Pour the mixture into each base.

Top with a lid, cook for 8 minutes, or until the crust is golden brown and crunchy.

Carefully remove and repeat.

CHICKEN PIE makes everyone HAPPY

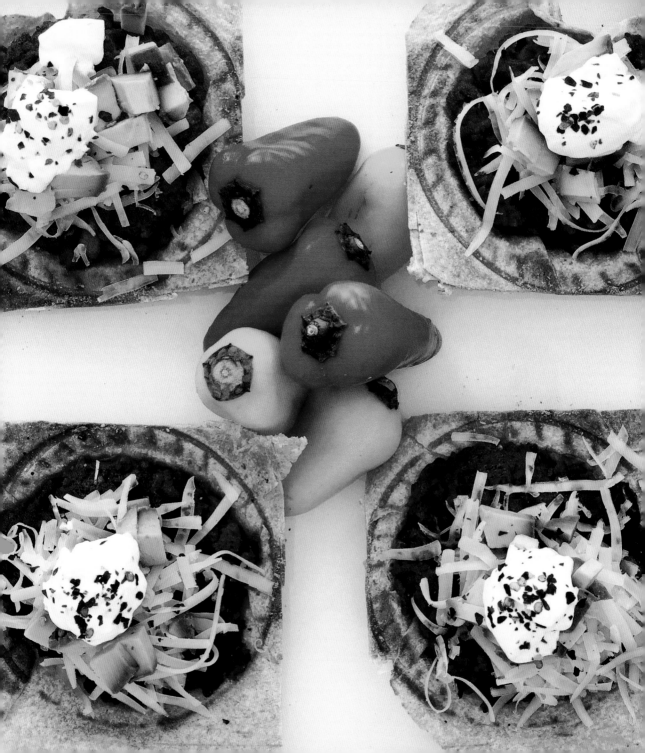

Chilli Con Carne Pies

Makes 8

A big batch of Chilli Con Carne can do so much. Serve it over rice, atop a hot spud or on a Pizza for dinner. Similarly, serve as part of a Chilli Cheese Dog, Chilli Cheese Nachos or Pies for lunch.

- 1 onion, peeled and chopped
- 1 garlic clove, crushed
- 500g lean beef mince
- 40g sachet Chilli Con Carne seasoning
- 1 tbsp. tomato paste

- 500g jar Chunky Vegetable Pasta sauce
- 400g can kidney beans, drained
- 1 tsp. Worcestershire sauce
- 8 small round wraps
- 1 cup grated cheddar cheese

Sauté onion for 2 minutes, add garlic and stir, sauté for 1 minute.

Add mince, using a fork, break up and cook stirring until browned, 6 minutes.

Add remaining ingredients (except wraps) and stir to combine.

Reduce heat and simmer for 20 to 30 minutes allowing time for flavours to develop.

Place the wraps in the microwave for 20 seconds to soften slightly then press into the holes of the Pie Maker.

Close the Pie Maker lid and cook for 3 minutes.

Scoop the mixture into the tortilla and cook for a further 7 minutes.

Carefully remove and top each pie with grated cheese.

OPTIONAL: Serve with a dollop of sour cream, diced avocado and a sprinkle of chilli flakes for a little extra bite.

Easy Mushroom Melts
Makes 8

- **8 large Portobello mushrooms**
- **3 tbsp. basil pesto**
- **½ cup grated mozzarella**
- **2 tbsp. pine nuts**

Wash and dry (or wipe) mushrooms.

Place the first 4 mushrooms into the pie holes, spoon over the basil pesto, sprinkle with mozzarella and pine nuts.

Close and cook for 5 minutes, or until cheese is golden brown.

Carefully remove and repeat.

Mushroom Pizzas
Makes 4

- 4 Portobello mushrooms
- 4 teaspoons Pizza sauce
- 4 cherry tomatoes
- ¼ red capsicum

- 12 English spinach leaves
- ½ cup grated mozzarella

Wash and dry (or wipe) mushrooms.

Remove the stems of the mushrooms and chop.

Place chopped stems in a bowl and add chopped tomatoes and capsicum.

Spread a teaspoon of pizza sauce across the underneath of each mushroom.

Add 3 spinach leaves and sprinkle with the vegetables. Season.

Top each mushroom with grated cheese.

Place each mushroom pizza into the pie holes.

Close and cook for 5 minutes, or until cheese is golden brown.

Maltese Pies
Makes 8 Small

- **4 eggs**
- **500g ricotta cheese**
- **¼ cup fresh chopped parsley**
- **3 sheets puff pastry**

In a bowl, whisk the eggs until light and fluffy, 2 minutes.

Add the ricotta and parsley and season well; mix to combine.

Cut 8 bases and 8 lids from the pastry sheets (using leftover pastry, join together, then roll out flat and thin).

Press the first 4 bases into the pie holes.

Pour the mixture into each base.

Top with a lid and garnish with a tendril of fresh parsley.

Close the lid and cook for 10 minutes, or until the crust is golden brown and crunchy.

Carefully remove and repeat.

Oodles of Noodles Pies
Makes 8 Large / 12 Small

- 2 rashers bacon, chopped
- 1 x 2-minute chicken noodle packet
- 4 eggs
- 2 shallots, finely chopped

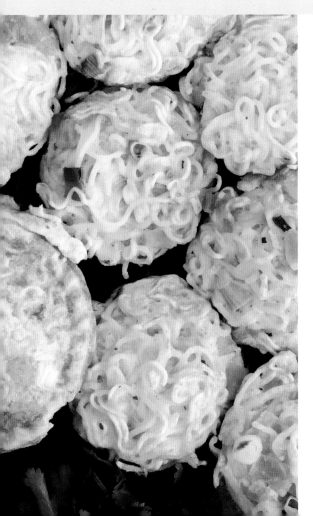

Sauté bacon until golden.

Empty the noodles into a bowl, cover with boiling water and sit for 4 minutes. Drain.

Add the chicken seasoning and stir to combine.

In a large bowl, whisk the eggs.

Add remaining ingredients and stir well.

Spoon enough mixture into each Pie Maker hole, level with the top.

Close the lid and cook for 10 minutes, or until the crust is golden brown and crunchy.

Carefully remove and repeat.

Mexican Brunch Pie
Makes 4

This divine recipe is from the Sunbeam Pie-oneer Digital Cookbook.

- 4 eggs
- 2 tbsp. pure cream
- 4 mini tortilla wraps
- 8 cherry tomatoes, cut in half

- ½ red onion, finely diced
- 1 chorizo, diced
- 3 tsp. dried chilli flakes (optional)
- ½ cup cheddar cheese, grated

In a bowl whisk eggs and cream,
season with salt and pepper.

Open Sunbeam Pie Magic® lid and
place a tortilla wrap in each pie hole.

Pour egg mixture into tortilla,
add tomato, onion, chorizo, chilli flakes
and cheese.

Close lid and turn on, cook for 15 minutes.

*OPTIONAL: Serve with sour cream,
avocado, jalapeños and fresh coriander.*

'I HATE MEXICAN'
SAID NO JUAN EVER!

Pizzas
Makes 4 Large / 6 Small

- **250g ball pizza dough (store-bought or homemade)**
- **¼ cup pizza paste**
- **1¼ cups shredded mozzarella cheese**

- **80g salami, roughly cut into 2cm squares**
- **Fresh basil leaves**

On a clean, floured surface, roll out dough until 5mm thick.

Use a 7cm round cutter to cut 8 rounds.

Turn on the Pie Maker.

Line the holes of the Pie Maker with dough rounds, the dough should come ¾ up the side of each hole.

Spread pizza sauce onto the bases. Sprinkle with a little of the mozzarella. Top each with salami and sprinkle with more cheese.

Bake for 10 to 12 minutes or until bases are golden and cheese is melted.

Serve warm sprinkled with fresh basil leaves.

2-Ingredient Pizza Dough

Mix 1½ cups self-raising flour with 1 cup Greek yoghurt together in a bowl. Transfer to a clean benchtop, floured with self-raising flour. Knead the dough, adding more flour as needed to keep the dough from being too sticky, 6 to 8 minutes.

Salmon & Asparagus Pies

Makes 4 Large

There are just some things that were made to be together. In the kitchen, they are ingredients like mint and chocolate, lamb and rosemary, strawberries and cream and salmon and asparagus.

- 6 eggs, whisked
- ¼ cup pure cream
- 1 tbsp. fresh dill, finely chopped
- 40g smoked salmon, torn

- 4 fresh asparagus spears, chopped
- 40g goat's cheese

In a jug, whisk together eggs and cream, season with sea salt and freshly cracked black pepper. Add dill.

Pour equal amounts of egg mixture into Sunbeam Pie Magic® dishes.

Add salmon, asparagus and goat's cheese.

Close lid, turn on and cook for 10 minutes.

Remove carefully, garnish with dill and a squeeze of fresh lemon juice.

Savoury Mince Pies
Makes 8 Large

This is one of those recipes that my Nana taught my Mum, my Mum taught me and I am now teaching my sons. Everyone should know how to make a basic Savoury Mince. Once you do, you can make Savoury Mince Rolls, Shepherd's Pies and these yummy pies to name a few.

- 1 onion, diced
- 500g lean beef mince
- 1 cup frozen mixed veggies
- 35g packet French onion soup

- 3 sheets puff pastry

Sauté onions in a non-stick frying pan over a medium heat until just soft, 4 minutes.

Add mince, using a fork, break up and cook stirring until browned, 6 minutes.

Add veggies, French onion soup and ½ cup water.

Season with cracked pepper.

Simmer for 10 minutes.

Meanwhile, lay the 3 sheets of puff pastry side by side (slightly overlapping).

Using a rolling pin, roll to connect.

Cut 8 bases and lids from the sheets (use the pastry offcuts too).

Place 4 bases of pastry into Pie Maker holes, fill with meat and top with pastry.

Close lid and cook for 10 minutes.

Carefully remove and repeat.

Spaghetti Cases
Makes 4 Large

- 4 slices multigrain bread
- 1 tbsp. butter
- 220g can spaghetti
- ½ cup grated cheddar cheese

Butter one side of each slice of bread.

Push the buttered side into each pie hole.

Spoon the spaghetti equally across each pie hole.

Sprinkle with grated cheese.

Close the lid and cook for 6 minutes or until golden.

Spaghetti Cupcakes
Makes 8 Small

- **4 eggs**
- **400g can spaghetti**
- **1½ cups grated cheddar cheese**

In a bowl, beat the eggs until light and fluffy, 2 minutes.

Add the cheese and the whole tin of spaghetti and mix to combine.

Using a ⅓ cup measure, fill each pie hole level with the machine.

Close and cook for 8 minutes.

Cool for 2 minutes before gently removing.

Repeat.

Thai Chicken Curry Pies
Makes 8 Large

- 1 onion, chopped
- ¼ cup green curry paste
- 270ml can coconut cream
- 800g chicken thigh fillets, cut into 2cm pieces
- 1 cup frozen, peas, corn and capsicum, thawed
- 2 tsp. cornflour
- 3 sheets frozen puff pastry

Sauté onion until golden, 4 minutes.

Add the green curry paste and stir.

Add the chicken and cook, tossing occasionally until sealed, 4 minutes.

Add the vegetables and season.

Pour over the coconut cream and stir to combine.

Reduce heat and simmer, 10 minutes.

Make a cornflour paste by mixing the cornflour into 2 tsp. cold water.

Add to the chicken and stir until nice and thick.

Meanwhile, lay the 3 sheets of puff pastry side by side (slightly overlapping).

Using a rolling pin, roll to connect.

Cut 8 bases and lids from the sheets (use the pastry offcuts too).

Place 4 bases of pastry into Pie Maker holes, fill with mixture and top with pastry.

Garnish the lid with a fresh coriander tendril.

Close lid and cook for 10 minutes.

Carefully remove and repeat.

Vegetarian Nacho Pies
Makes 8 Large / 12 Small

- 400g can mixed beans, drained
- 1 cup grated cheddar cheese
- ⅓ cup chopped shallots
- 1 medium red capsicum, finely chopped
- 2 puff pastry sheets
- 1 handful tortilla chips
- 2 tbsp. chopped coriander
- 8 jalapeños, chopped

Mix beans, cheese, shallots and capsicum in a bowl. Set aside.

Pre-heat Pie Maker.

Cut out 12 pie bases.

Line the pie holes with pastry.

Crush a few tortilla chips in each base then fill with the beans mixture.

Sprinkle with coriander and a few jalapeños; use more if you like it spicy.

Close and cook for 15 minutes.

Remove pies and cool slightly.

Serve with more crushed tortillas and a dollop of salsa and sour cream or your Guacamole.

Guacamole

Dice ¼ red onion, 1 small vine-ripened tomato and an avocado. Place all into a bowl and season with ¼ cup freshly chopped coriander, sea salt and cracked pepper. Serve immediately or cover well and refrigerate.

Zucchini Slice Pies

Makes 8 Small

These pies are everyone's favourites; a real crowd-pleaser. They are gluten free, fresh, light and lovely, make them to the delight of all.

- **2 zucchinis, grated**
- **4 eggs**
- **1 tsp. curry powder**
- **½ cup (125g) sour cream**

- **3 tbsp. grated Parmesan**

Gently squeeze excess liquid from the zucchinis.

In a bowl, whisk the eggs, add the curry powder and sour cream and whisk again.

Add the zucchini and half the Parmesan and stir well.

Lightly brush the pie holes with oil.

Fill with ⅓ cup mixture.

Lay a round zucchini slice on the top of each and season.

Close lid and cook for 8 minutes.

DINNER
PIES

Aussie Mince Pies

Makes 8 Large / 12 Small

- 1 large onion, finely chopped
- 700g beef mince
- 400g can crushed tomatoes
- ¾ cup beef stock

- 3 tbsp. Worcestershire sauce
- 2 tbsp. BBQ sauce
- 2 tbsp. cornflour
- 4 puff pastry sheets

Sauté onions in a non-stick frying pan over a medium heat until just soft, 4 minutes.

Add mince, using a fork, break up and cook stirring until browned, 6 minutes.

Add tomatoes, beef stock, Worcestershire and BBQ sauces and stir to combine.

Bring to a gentle boil then reduce heat and simmer for 20 minutes, or until liquid has reduced by half.

Combine cornflour with 2 tbsp. cold water, stirring until smooth.

Increase heat and gradually add the cornflour paste to the mince stirring continuously, until the mixture thickens.

Meanwhile, lay the 4 sheets of puff pastry side by side (slightly overlapping). Using a rolling pin, roll to connect.

Cut 8 bases and lids from the sheets.

Place 4 bases of pastry into Pie Maker, fill with meat and top with pastry.

Close lid and cook for 8 to 10 minutes.

Carefully remove and repeat.

OPTIONAL: You could add a little mashed potato or mushy peas, on top of the meat mixture, before you pop the lid on. However in our house, we love these pies as is with mashed potato and peas on the side.

Beef & Ale Pies

Makes 8 Large

- 1kg beef steak, cubed
- ½ cup (75g) plain flour
- 2 tbsp. butter
- 2 onions, peeled and chopped
- 2 stalks celery, trimmed and chopped
- 2 carrots, chopped
- 1 garlic clove, crushed
- 2 cups (500ml) beef stock
- 200ml pale ale
- 4 puff pastry sheets

Coat the beef in flour and season well with sea salt and cracked pepper.

Place a non-stick frying pan over high heat.

Add half the butter and swirl to coat.

Fry the beef in 2 batches until sealed. Remove from the pan and set aside.

Melt remaining butter over a medium heat.

Add the onion, celery, carrot and garlic and sauté, 3 minutes or until softened.

Add the beef, then pour in the stock and ale (the beef should be just covered).

Bring to the boil, stirring and skimming off any fat that rises to the surface.

Lower the heat, cover and simmer for 1 hour or until the beef is tender.

When ready, cut 8 bases and lids from the sheets (use the pastry offcuts too).

Place 4 bases of pastry into Pie Maker, fill with meat and top with pastry.

Close lid and cook for 10 minutes.

Carefully remove and repeat.

OPTIONAL: Sprinkle the lid with poppy seeds before cooking.

A Steak Pun
is a rare medium well done.

Bolognese Baskets
Makes 6 Small

- 2 puff pastry sheets
- 2 cups Bolognese sauce
- 1 cup baby spinach
- 12 fresh basil leaves

- 1 cup grated mozzarella cheese

Cut 6 rounds of puff pastry.

Cut the remaining pastry into 1cm strips.

Line each pie hole with pastry, fill with Bolognese, spinach, basil and mozzarella in that order.

To create the basket look, use the strips of pastry to form a criss-cross pattern on top of each pie.

Close the lid and cook for 8 minutes.

Carefully remove and repeat.

Bolognese Scrolls

A family favourite from 4 Ingredients KIDS. Preheat oven 180ºC. Line a baking tray with baking paper. Onto a sheet of puff pastry, spoon Bolognese sauce. Top with fresh baby spinach and grated Parmesan. Season. Roll. Slice. Bake 25 to 30 minutes or until golden and puffed.

Cauliflower, Cheese & Spinach Pies
Makes 8 Small

- ½ cauliflower, florets removed
- 40g butter
- 2 cups milk
- 3 tablespoons plain flour
- ½ cup grated cheddar cheese

- 4 tablespoons grated pecorino (or Parmesan) cheese
- Small bag (60g) baby spinach
- 3 puff pastry sheets

Steam cauliflower until tender.

Meanwhile, to make the cheese sauce, gently melt the butter in a frying pan.

In a jug, whisk milk and flour together well.

Pour into pan when butter is bubbling and stir constantly until the mixture thickens.

Reduce heat, add cheeses and spinach, season and stir.

Chop the cooled cauliflower and add to the cheese mixture. Season.

Cut 8 bases and lids from the sheets.

Place 4 bases of pastry into Pie Maker, fill with mixture and top with pastry.

Close lid and cook for 8 minutes.

Carefully remove and repeat.

Chicken & Veggie Pies
Makes 8 Small

- ½ BBQ chicken
- 2 cups frozen mixed vegetables, thawed (and drained of excess liquid)
- 400g can condensed cream of chicken soup

- 3 puff pastry sheets

Into a bowl, shred the chicken, pulling it into fine pieces (approx. 2 cups).

Add the drained veggies and season with cracked pepper.

Add the soup and mix to combine.

Cut 8 bases and 8 lids from the sheets.

Press the first 4 bases into the pie holes.

Spoon the mixture into each base.

Top with a lid and sprinkle with some peas and corn.

Close and cook for 8 minutes, or until the crust is golden brown and crunchy.

Carefully remove and repeat.

OPTIONAL: Season lid with fresh thyme as well as cracked pepper.

Perfectly Formed Pies

Remember the first tip from p. 9? To ensure perfectly rounded, golden pies, pop enough filling into each pie hole so that when the lid is added, it touches the top of the Pie Maker.

Chicken Carbonara Pies
Makes 8 Large / 12 Small

WELL THESE WERE A HIT! My 12-year old declared them 'The best pies ever!'

- 200g bacon, diced
- 500g chicken thighs, chopped
- 500ml cream thickened
- 1 cup grated 3-cheese mix

- 4 tsp. wholegrain mustard
- 2 tsp. cornflour (mixed 2 tsp. cold water)
- 4 puff pastry sheets

In a large frying pan over medium heat, cook the bacon until golden, 3 minutes.

Add the chicken and season.

Cook, stirring, until browned.

Lower the heat and add the cream, cheeses and mustard.

Simmer and stir until the cheese has melted, 2 minutes.

Add the cornflour paste and stir until the filling thickens to desired consistency.

Cut 12 bases and 12 lids from the pastry sheets (using leftover pastry, join together, then roll out flat and thin).

Press the first 4 bases into the pie holes.

Spoon the mixture into each base.

Top with a lid and a light brush of wholegrain mustard.

Close and cook for 8 to 10 minutes, or until the crust is golden brown and crunchy.

Carefully remove and repeat.

OPTIONAL: Add a little chopped shallot or parsley to the chicken mixture if you have it. I can't help myself, I tend to add green to everything.

Creamy Bacon, Semi-dried Tomatoes & Chicken Pies

Makes 6 Large

- 200g bacon, diced
- 500g chicken thighs, chopped
- ⅓ cup semi-dried tomatoes, chopped
- 2 shallots, chopped

- 250ml Cream for Cooking (or cream)
- 3 puff pastry sheets

In a large frying pan over medium heat, sauté the bacon, stirring, for 4 minutes.

Add the chicken and cook in the bacon oil, tossing until golden.

Add the semi-dried tomatoes and shallots, stir to combine.

Lower the heat and add the cream.

Simmer for 5 minutes or until the sauce has thickened slightly.

Cut 8 bases and 8 lids from the pastry sheets (using leftover pastry, join together, then roll out flat and thin).

Press the first 4 bases into the pie holes.

Pour the mixture into each base.

Top with a lid, close and cook for 10 minutes, or until the crust is golden brown and crunchy.

Carefully remove and repeat.

YOU WANT A PIECE of me?

Fish Pies
Makes 8 Small

This recipe comes from a gorgeous girlfriend of mine Kerry Phairs. We seem to chat endlessly about yummy recipes and this was one of hers I'm forever GRATEFUL for.

- 800g frozen mixed vegetables, thawed
- 2 tbsp. plain flour
- 400g skinless smoked cod, trout or salmon, 3cm pieces
- 1½ cups (375ml) fish stock
- 3 puff pastry sheets

In a non-stick frying pan over medium heat, sauté the veggies for 8 minutes or until soft and starting to brown.

Sprinkle over flour and stir cooking for 1 minute or until well coated.

Add the stock and fish and stir until well combined.

Reduce heat and simmer for 10 minutes.

Season to taste.

Cut 8 bases and 8 lids from the pastry sheets (using leftover pastry, join together, then roll out flat and thin).

Press the first 4 bases into the pie holes.

Pour the mixture into each base.

Top with a lid, close and cook for 8 minutes, or until the crust is golden brown and crunchy.

Carefully remove and repeat.

Kiwi Pies

Makes 6 Large / 8 Small

Straight from the kitchens of my good friends in New Zealand. According to Craig Wilson, 'There would be very few Kiwis who have not eaten a good ole Mince 'n' Cheese Pie! I reckon it's one of the things we'd take with us if we were going to be stranded on a desert island!'

- 1 onion, chopped
- 500g lean beef mince
- 2 tbsp. freshly chopped parsley
- 1½ cups (380ml) beef stock
- 1 tbsp. cornflour
- 200g grated tasty cheddar cheese
- 3 puff pastry sheets

Sauté onion in a non-stick frying pan over a medium heat until just soft, 4 minutes.

Add mince, using a fork, break up and cook stirring until browned, 6 minutes.

Season generously with sea salt and cracked pepper and cook for 8 minutes or until brown.

Add parsley and beef stock and stir to combine.

Reduce heat and simmer for 20 minutes.

Mix the cornflour with 1 tbsp. cold water until nice and smooth.

Add to mince and stir to combine until the mixture thickens.

Cut 8 bases and 8 lids from the pastry sheets (using leftover pastry, join together, then roll out flat and thin).

Press the first 4 bases into the pie holes.

Pour the mixture into each base.

Top with a lid, close and cook for 8 minutes, or until the crust is golden brown and crunchy.

Carefully remove and repeat.

Lamb Korma Pies
Makes 8 Small

- 1 onion, chopped
- 500g lamb mince
- ¼ cup sultanas
- 400ml Korma sauce

- 60g fresh baby spinach
- 3 puff pastry sheets

Sauté onion in a non-stick frying pan over a medium heat until just soft, 4 minutes.

Add mince, using a fork, break up and cook stirring until browned, 4 minutes.

Drain excess fat, sauté for another 2 minutes, drain excess fat.

Add the sultanas and sauce.

Cover and simmer for 20 minutes, allowing time for the yummy flavours to develop together.

In the last 5 minutes add the spinach and stir to combine.

Cut 8 bases and 8 lids from the pastry sheets (using leftover pastry, join together, then roll out flat and thin).

Press the first 4 bases into the pie holes.

Spoon the mixture into each.

Top with a lid, close and cook for 8 minutes, or until the crust is golden brown and crunchy.

Carefully remove and repeat.

OPTIONAL: Serve with a dollop of Mango Chutney.

Lasagne
Makes 4 Large

Lasagne in a Pie Maker, isn't that clever? Not my idea, but one I have borrowed many times since first seeing it in the Sunbeam Pie-oneer Digital Cookbook.

- **2 fresh lasagne sheets, cut into 16 squares**
- **1 cup bolognese sauce**
- **¾ cup white béchamel sauce**

- **½ cup cheddar cheese, grated**

Place one lasagne square into the base of each of the Sunbeam Pie Magic® dishes.

Add 2 tablespoons of bolognese, 1 tablespoon white béchamel sauce and top with lasagne sheet.

Repeat twice with 1 tablespoon bolognese sauce, 1 tablespoon béchamel sauce and lasagne square, then finish with 1 tablespoon béchamel sauce, and grated cheese.

Close lid, turn on and cook for 15 minutes.

Allow lasagne to sit and cool for 5 minutes.

Carefully remove and repeat.

OPTIONAL: Serve sprinkled with fresh basil leaves and a side of fresh salad greens.

Basic Béchamel

Melt 60g butter in a saucepan over medium heat until foaming. Add ⅓ cup flour and stir, cooking for 1 to 2 minutes. Slowly add 4 cups milk, whisking constantly, until mixture is smooth and thick. Add ¾ cup grated Parmesan and season with a good pinch of sea salt and nutmeg.

Pulled Pork Pies
Makes 4 Large

When I first saw this image in the Sunbeam Pie-oneer Digital Cookbook, my heart skipped a beat. I knew immediately this was a pie my three sons would love ... and they did (still do)!

- 2 cups pulled pork, warm
- 4 tbsp. pickled jalapeños (optional)
- ½ cup kale coleslaw
- 1 cup mozzarella cheese, grated

- 3 puff pastry sheets

Turn Sunbeam Pie Magic® on and preheat.

In a large bowl mix leftover pulled pork, jalapeños, kale coleslaw and cheese.

Using the pastry cutter provided, cut out 4 bases and 4 tops.

Overlap the base flaps, making a pastry shell.

Place the pastry shells in each pie hole, top each pie with the pulled pork mixture and add pastry lid on top, brush with whisked egg.

Close lid and cook for 14 minutes, or until pastry is golden brown.

Pumpkin & Lentil Pies
Makes 4 Large / 6 Small

- **2 tbsp. red curry paste**
- **300g pumpkin, peeled and chopped**
- **400ml can coconut milk**
- **400g can brown lentils, drained**

- **2 puff pastry sheets**

In a non-stick frying pan, add the red curry paste and fry over a medium heat for 20 seconds.

Add the pumpkin and toss to coat well.

Add the coconut milk and stir.

Bring to a gentle boil, reduce heat, simmering for 10 minutes, then add the lentils.

Simmer for another 10 minutes or until tender.

Cut 4 bases and 4 lids from the pastry sheets (using leftover pastry, join together, then roll out flat and thin).

Press 4 bases into the pie holes.

Spoon the mixture evenly across each.

Top with a lid, close and cook for 8 to 10 minutes, or until the crust is golden brown and crunchy.

Carefully remove and repeat.

OPTIONAL: Serve with Pappadums or Naan bread. Similarly, lay a fresh sage leaf across the lid of each pie before cooking. I love the pairing of pumpkin and sage.

Shepherd's Pies

Makes 6 Large

- 500g lean beef (or lamb) mince
- ¾ cup fruit chutney
- 2 cups mashed potatoes
- 6 slices wholemeal bread, crusts removed

In a large non-stick frying pan brown the mince, stirring to break it up.

Add the chutney and stir to combine.

Reduce heat and simmer for 15 minutes.

When ready, press the bread slices into pie holes.

Spoon the mixture into each.

Top each with ⅓ cup mashed potato.

Season lightly.

Close the lid and cook for 8 minutes, or until crust is golden brown and top has formed a slight crust.

OPTIONAL: I have made these often, they are the perfect veggie smuggler, so into the mince grate carrot, parsnip, zucchini, chop onions, capsicums and fresh parsley. Just allow time for the veggies to cook when simmering.

Total
COMFORT
FOOD

Spinach, Ricotta & Feta Pies
Makes 8

- 3 shallots
- ½ cup parsley
- 200g packet baby spinach leaves
- 200g feta cheese

- 3 large eggs, lightly beaten
- 750g ricotta cheese
- 2 sheets of puff pastry

Finely chop shallots and parsley and roughly chop the spinach.

Crumble the feta.

In a large bowl, whisk the eggs and the ricotta, season and mix to combine.

Add remaining ingredients and mix together.

Cut 8 bases from the pastry sheets.

Press the first 4 bases into the pie holes.

Spoon the mixture evenly across each.

Close and cook for 8 to 10 minutes, or until the crust is golden brown and crunchy.

Carefully remove and repeat.

Simple Greek Salad

In a serving bowl combine 4 cherry tomatoes halved, 4 Cukes chopped, 2 tbsp. finely diced red onion, ⅓ cup pitted Kalamata olives, 60g crumbled feta and a sprinkling of fresh parsley. Season and serve drizzled with fresh lemon juice.

Steak & Mushroom Pies
Makes 6 Large

- 600g beef steak, cubed
- ⅓ cup (50g) plain flour, well seasoned
- 3 tbsp. olive oil
- 2 onions, sliced

- 2 cups (500ml) beef stock
- 120g mushrooms, sliced
- 3 sheets puff pastry

Toss meat in seasoned flour, then fry in hot oil in small batches until browned.

Stir in onions and cook for 2 minutes, stirring.

Gradually add the beef stock, and bring to the boil, stirring frequently until the sauce thickens slightly.

Lower the heat, cover and simmer for 1 hour or until the beef is nice and tender.

Add mushrooms, stir and simmer for 20 minutes or until nice and tender.

Bring to the boil, skimming off any fat that rises to the surface.

When ready, cut 8 bases and lids from the sheets (use the pastry offcuts too).

Place 4 bases of pastry into Pie Maker, fill with meat and top with pastry. Scatter a few slices of mushroom over the lid.

Close lid and cook for 10 minutes.

Carefully remove and repeat.

STEAK *makes us* HAPPY!

ENTERTAINING

Halloumi Stacks
Makes 12

- 180g halloumi cheese
- 12 cherry tomatoes
- 12 Kalamata olives, pitted
- 12 basil leaves

Preheat Pie Maker. Cut the halloumi into 4 long strips, then each strip into thirds. Pop the first 4 squares into pie holes. Close lid and cook 2 minutes. Flip, cook for another 2 minutes, or until golden. Carefully remove and repeat. To serve, top each square with tomato, olive and fresh basil leaf and stud with a toothpick to hold together.

Parmesan Crisps
Makes 12

- **1 cup grated Parmesan cheese**

Sprinkle the base of the Pie Maker with Parmesan, covering generously. Close lid and cook for 4 minutes. Turn off and cool, 4 minutes. Carefully remove by slipping a fork underneath the crisp. Repeat.

Spinach Cob
Makes 6

- 250g sour cream
- 35g packet Spring Vegetable soup
- 200g frozen spinach, thawed (squeeze to remove excess liquid)
- 6 small dinner rolls

Into a bowl, place sour cream and spring vegetable soup and mix to combine. Season with cracked pepper. Add spinach and stir well. Cut the lid from each small roll and tear out ⅔ the filling, leaving a soft plum wall. Spoon the spinach mixture into each roll. Place in pie holes, close lid and cook for 6 minutes. Open, add lid and cook for 2 minutes more. Carefully remove and repeat.

SWEET PIES

Apple Anzac Pies
Makes 8 Small

- ½ cup quick oats
- 2 tbsp. cinnamon sugar
- 2 tbsp. desiccated coconut
- 4 tbsp. (60g) butter, melted

- 400g can pie apple
- 3 sheets shortcrust pastry

In a bowl, place oats, cinnamon sugar, coconut and melted butter; season with sea salt and stir to combine.

Cut 8 bases from the pastry sheets.

Press 4 bases into the pie holes.

Dollop ⅓ cup of pie apple into each, top with a generous spoonful of oat mixture.

Turn Pie Maker on, close lid and cook for 8 minutes.

Remove carefully and repeat.

Apple Crumble Pies

A variation of the above is to crumble into a bowl 8 Scotch Finger biscuits. Stir in 4 tbsp. melted butter. Line each pie hole with pastry. Fill with stewed apple and sprinkle with prepared crumble. Turn Pie Maker on, close lid and cook for 7 minutes.

Baked Lemon Cheesecakes
Makes 6 Small

- 250g cream cheese, softened
- ⅓ cup Natvia
- 2 eggs
- 1 lemon, zest and 2 tbsp. juice

- 6 butternut snap cookies

Using a handheld beater, mix together cream cheese and Natvia until nice and smooth.

Add eggs, lemon zest and juice and beat again, 1 minute.

Lightly grease each pie hole with a little melted butter or coconut oil.

Place a Buttersnap biscuit (flat side up) in each pie hole, then pour approx. ¼ cup measure of mixture into each.

Turn Pie Maker on, close lid and cook for 8 minutes.

Turn off heat and cool.

Carefully remove and repeat with remaining ingredients.

OPTIONAL: Serve with a splash of fresh berries; strawberries, blueberries or raspberries. Whatever is in season.

Banoffee Pies

Makes 8

Banoffee pie gets its name from a combination of toffee and bananas. Insanely delicious, these are the quickest, easiest little pies you will ever make.

- 2 shortcrust pastry sheets
- 395g can Caramel Top 'n' Fill
- 1 cup whipped cream
- 1 banana, sliced into rounds

Cut 8 rounds from the pastry
(we used a flower shaped cutter).

Push the first 4 into the Pie Maker
and gently mould into the pie holes.

Close the lid and cook for 6 minutes.

Cool, carefully remove and repeat.

Meanwhile, in a bowl, beat the
caramel until nice and smooth.

Spoon it into the bases.

Chill until needed.

Just before serving, dollop with
whipped cream and a slice of banana.

*OPTIONAL: To serve, top with a sprinkling of
grated chocolate and a pretty little flower.*

Beetroot Cupcakes
Makes 10 Small

Here's the thing, my husband doesn't like beetroot, so I told him they were strawberry cupcakes. It wasn't until after he'd devoured two, that I confessed ... He couldn't believe it!

- **340g packet vanilla cake mix**
- **275g can beetroot, drained and puréed**
- **¾ cup soda water**

In a large bowl, whisk the cake mix. Create a well, add beetroot and soda water. Gently fold to combine.

Pour ⅓ cup of mixture into each pie hole. Turn Pie Maker on, close lid and cook for 8 minutes or until the centre springs back when gently pressed.

Carefully remove and repeat.

Eat as is, or with a delicious buttercream frosting see p. 117. But rather than cocoa powder, use the juice of the beetroot for flavour and natural colour instead.

If at first you don't succeed
EAT A CUPCAKE

Banana Muffins
Makes 12 Small

- **2 ripe bananas**
- **¼ cup caster sugar (or Natvia)**
- **½ cup whole-egg mayonnaise**
- **1 cup self-raising flour**

Preheat the Pie Maker.

In a bowl, mash the bananas.

Add the sugar, mayonnaise and 2 tbsp. water and stir to combine.

Add the flour and gently fold to combine.

Set aside for 4 minutes.

Drop ¼ cup measure of mixture into each pie hole.

Close lid and cook for 8 minutes.

Carefully remove and repeat.

OPTIONAL: Before closing, sprinkle each with ground cinnamon and nutmeg and top with a banana round.

Cherry Pies
Makes 8 Small

- 420g can pitted cherries in syrup
- 1/3 cup mixed berry jam
- 2 tbsp. Natvia
- 1½ tbsp. cornflour

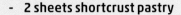

- 2 sheets shortcrust pastry

Pour contents of cherries into a saucepan.

Add the jam and sugar and over a medium heat, stir until the sugar and jam have dissolved.

Make a cornflour paste with cornflour and 1½ tbsp. cold water, stirring until nice and smooth.

Add to the cherries and stir until nice and thick, 4 minutes.

Set aside and cool slightly.

Using a pastry cutter, cut 8 small rounds from the pastry.

Line the first 4 pie holes with pastry rounds.

Fill with cherry mixture.

Turn Pie Maker on, close lid and cook for 8 minutes.

Carefully remove and repeat.

OPTIONAL: Serve each with a dollop of double cream.

Chocolate Zucchini Cupcakes
Makes 10 Small

- 340g packet chocolate cake mix
- 1 cup grated zucchini
- 1 cup soda water

In a large bowl, whisk the cake mix.

Create a well, add zucchini and soda water.

Gently fold to combine.

Pour ⅓ cup of mixture into each pie hole.

Turn Pie Maker on, close lid and cook for 8 minutes or until the centre springs back when gently pressed.

Carefully remove and repeat.

Eat as is, or with a delicious buttercream frosting.

5-Minute Chocolate Buttercream Frosting

Using a hand-held beater, beat 5 tbsp. soft butter for 1 minute until nice and smooth. Add 2 cups icing sugar, ½ cup cocoa powder and beat for 3 minutes, scraping down the sides as needed. Gradually add 2 tbsp. milk and continue to beat for 1 minute. **OPTIONAL:** Add 1 tsp. vanilla extract and a pinch of sea salt.

Custard Fruit Pies
Makes 6 Large

This yummy recipe is a variation of our Vanilla Slice, which thanks to you, has been shared from our Facebook page over 24,000 times!

- 100g packet Cottees Vanilla Dessert Mix
- 600ml thickened cream
- 12 slices raisin bread, crusts removed
- 3 tbsp. soft butter

In a large bowl, use a hand-held beater to combine the dessert mix and cream, mix until well combined, 1 minute.

Cover and refrigerate for 15 minutes.

Using a rolling pin, roll each slice of bread to flatten slightly, then butter one only.

Press the first 4 slices, butter side down, into the pie holes.

Remove dessert mix from refrigerator and stir until nice and smooth.

Pour ⅓ cup of mixture into each.

Top with slice of raisin bread, buttered side up.

Turn Pie Maker on, close lid and cook for 8 minutes.

Allow to cool slightly, then remove and repeat.

Custard Tarts / Makes 8

- 2 sheets of Shortcrust pastry
- 500ml custard, ready made
- 1 egg, beaten
- ½ tsp. vanilla essence
- 1 tsp. nutmeg

Cut out 4 bases. Cook for 4 minutes or until golden. Mix together custard, egg and vanilla essence. Spoon into pastry cases, sprinkle with ground nutmeg and cook for 8 minutes.

Donuts

Makes 8

This lovely recipe came to us via a long-time friend of 4 Ingredients, Cassandra Van Bruegel from Chattanooga, Tennessee, USA.

- 340g packet vanilla cake mix
- 1 egg, beaten
- ½ cup water
- ¼ cup vegetable oil

- 4 tbsp. cinnamon sugar

In a bowl, whisk the cake mix.

Make a well in the centre and add the egg, water and vegetable oil.

Gently fold to combine.

Pour ⅓ cup of mixture into each pie hole.

Turn Pie Maker on, close lid and cook for 4 minutes.

Carefully flip and cook for another 4 minutes.

Remove and use an apple corer to cut an inside circle from the cake.

Whilst hot, dust generously with cinnamon sugar before serving.

OPTIONAL: Leave whole, cut in half, spread with Nutella or Strawberry Jam before rolling in cinnamon sugar.

FunFetti Cupcakes

Makes 8 Small

These are a variation of our 2-Ingredient Cupcakes first published in 4 Ingredients KIDS in 2012. On a promotional trip to America, we discovered FunFetti Cakes where they simply add 100s & 1000s to a vanilla cake mix. Fun to make, fun to decorate and fun to eat.

- 340g packet Vanilla Cake mix
- 2 tbsp. 100s & 1000s
- 1 cup soda water

In a large bowl, mix together cake mix and 100s & 1000s.

Slowly pour in the soda water gently folding with a large spoon or spatula, until just combined. Do not over fold.

Pour ⅓ cup of mixture into each pie hole.

Turn Pie Maker on, close lid and cook for 8 minutes or until just golden and the centre springs back when gently pressed.

Cool before icing.

Rose Buttercream Frosting

- 2 tbsp. softened butter
- 1 cup icing sugar
- 1 tbsp. milk (or cream)
- 4 drops Rose colouring

Cook Beat the butter until pale, 1 minute. Add the icing sugar and continue to mix well, 3 minutes. Add milk and rose colouring and mix to combine. Use to ice when cupcakes have cooled. Serve sprinkled with 100s & 1000s.

Impossible Pies
Makes 8 Large / 12 Small

The Impossible Pie is named as such not because it is impossible to make, quite the contrary, but more because all its ingredients go into one bowl and magically separate into a top, bottom and filling layer while baking. The layers are not as pronounced when baked in a Pie Maker, but nonetheless delicious.

- 4 eggs
- ½ cup butter melted
- ½ cup (60g) plain flour
- ¾ cup (150g) caster sugar

- 1 cup (110g) desiccated coconut
- 2 cups milk
- 2 tsp. vanilla essence
- Nutmeg to sprinkle

Preheat pie machine.

In a bowl, whisk the eggs until light and fluffy.

Add remaining ingredients, and stir to combine.

Pour ⅓ cup of mixture into each pie hole.

Close lid and cook for 10 minutes.

Cool slightly before removing carefully and repeating.

Iced Vo-Vo Tarts
Makes 8 Small

- 2 sheets shortcrust pastry
- 8 tsp. raspberry (or strawberry) jam
- 100g marshmallows
- 20g pouring cream

- 3 tbsp. desiccated coconut

Cut 8 bases from the pastry.

Line the first 4 holes with pastry rounds.

Turn Pie Maker on, close lid and cook for 6 minutes.

Carefully remove and repeat.

Meanwhile, in the microwave, melt the marshmallows and cream on low for 30 seconds and stir until smooth.

Add a teaspoon of jam into the base of each shell and top with marshmallow mixture.

Sprinkle with coconut.

Pop into an airtight container and refrigerate for 30 minutes to set.

These are the
REASON
we ♥ our
Pie Maker

Key Lime Pies
Makes 8 Small

- 4 large egg yolks
- 400g can condensed milk
- 4 limes, juiced and 2 tsp. zest
- 2 sheets shortcrust pastry

Using an electric mixer, beat the egg yolks until they are thick and turn pale yellow.

Gradually add the condensed milk.

Stir in half the lime juice. Once incorporated, add the other half plus 2 tsp. lime zest and stir to combine.

Cut 8 bases from shortcrust pastry.

Press the first 4 sheets into the pie holes.

Pour lime filling evenly into each.

Close and cook for 10 minutes or until the filling is set.

Carefully remove and repeat.

OPTIONAL: Serve with a dollop of whipped cream. Use the egg whites to make Friands on p. 135, or a yummy Pavlova.

Pavlova

I have made Mini-pavs in a Pie Maker but I find it much easier to create one big Pavlova and bake it in the oven. Using a stand mixer, beat 4 egg whites until soft peaks form. Gradually add 1 cup caster sugar, beating continuously until thick and glossy, 10 minutes. Fold in 1 tbsp. cornflour, then ½ tsp. white vinegar until just combined. Preheat oven 130ºC. Line a baking tray with baking paper. Pile the meringue into a 20cm diameter circle. Cook in lower half of oven. Bake for 15 minutes, reduce heat to 100ºC and bake for 1¼ hours. Turn off the oven and let the pavlova cool completely with the door ajar.

Lemington Cakes

Makes 8

- 340g packet vanilla cake mix
- 1 cup lemon Solo
- $^2/_3$ cup lemon curd
- 2 cups desiccated coconut

- 300ml thickened cream, whipped

Place the cake mix into a bowl.

Slowly pour in the Solo, gently folding with a large spoon or spatula, until just combined. Do not over fold.

Pour $^1/_3$ cup of mixture into each pie hole.

Cook for 8 minutes.

Carefully remove from Pie Maker and cool slightly.

Repeat.

Cut cakes in half and spread the outsides entirely in lemon curd.

Sprinkle the cakes well with desiccated coconut.

Spread each cake base with whipped cream and sandwich together to serve.

Carefully remove and repeat.

LIFE *is short* *eat the* CAKE

Pecan Pies
Makes 6 Small

- 4 tbsp. (60g) butter, melted
- 1 cup brown sugar
- ¼ cup golden syrup
- 2 eggs

- 240g pecans
- 2 sheets shortcrust pastry

In a bowl, combine well the butter, sugar, syrup and eggs.

Add the pecans and a pinch of sea salt and mix well.

Cut out 6 base rounds from pastry.

Line each pie hole with pastry, gently press to mould.

Pour ⅓ cup of mixture into each.

Bake for 10 minutes.

Carefully remove and repeat.

Pumpkin Pies
Makes 8 Small

- 2 large eggs
- 1 cup creamy vanilla ice-cream
- 1 cup pumpkin purée
- 2 shortcrust pastry sheets

In a bowl, whisk the eggs really well or until pale and frothy.

Add the ice-cream and pumpkin purée and mix well.

Cut 8 bases from the pastry.

Press the first 4 into the pie holes.

Pour in ⅓ cup of filling.

Close and cook for 10 minutes.

OPTIONAL: Serve dusted with a little icing sugar.

Raspberry & White Chocolate Friands
Makes 8 Large

- 3 egg whites
- ²/₃ cup pure icing sugar
- ²/₃ cup almond meal
- 2 tbsp. plain flour

- 100g butter, melted
- 1 tsp. vanilla extract
- ¹/₃ cup frozen raspberries, thawed
- ¹/₃ cup chopped white chocolate

Using hand-held beaters, beat the egg whites until soft peaks form.

In a large bowl, whisk icing sugar, almond meal and plain flour to combine.

Once cooled, add the butter into the mix.

Then add vanilla extract and egg whites and whisk until combined.

Carefully stir through the berries and white chocolate.

Pre-heat the Sunbeam Pie Magic® and wait for the green light.

Pour ¹/₃ cup of mixture into each pie hole.

Close the Pie Maker and cook for 10 minutes.

Cool slightly before removing.

Repeat.

Snow Cakes
Makes 6 Large / 8 Small

We all know the 'Snow Cake' phenomenon that swept the internet last year, everywhere I looked there they were. But it was the absolute simplicity of this Sunbeam Pie-oneer Digital Cookbook image that took my breath away.

- **340g vanilla cake mix**
- **1 cup soda water**
- **½ cup strawberry jam**
- **1 cup whipped cream**
- **½ cup icing sugar, dusting**

Place the cake mix into a bowl.

Slowly pour in the soda water, gently folding with a large spoon or spatula, until just combined. Do not over fold.

Open lid of the Sunbeam Pie Magic® and pour batter evenly into each pie hole.

Close lid, turn on and cook for 10 minutes.

Use a cake skewer to check if cake is cooked through. Place on a cooling rack and wait for cakes to cool.

With a serrated knife, cut cakes in half and dust with icing sugar using a sifter.

Spread with jam and cream, then sandwich together.

Repeat.

when you share a **SNOW CAKE** *you share* **LOVE**

SO MANY PIES

SO FEW PAGES

Please Join Us

4 Ingredients is a family of busy people bound together by the desire to create good, healthy, homemade meals quickly, easily and economically.

Our aim is to save us all precious time and money in the kitchen. If this is you too, then we invite you to join our growing family where we share kitchen wisdom daily.

Similarly, if you have a favourite recipe or a tip that has worked for you in the kitchen and think others would enjoy it too, we'd love to hear from you:

 facebook.com/4ingredientspage

4 Ingredients Channel

 @4ingredients

 @4ingredients

 @4ingredients

 4ingredients.com.au

Bibliography

Websites

Recipes
www.4ingredients.com.au/recipes

New Idea Food
www.newideafood.com.au

Nutritional Information
www.foodworks.com.au

Sunbeam Pie Maker Group
www.facebook.com/sunbeampiemakergroup

Sunbeam Pie-oneer Digital Cookbook
https://www.sunbeam.com.au/en/content/
piemaker-recipes/

Kmart Pie Maker Recipes, Tips & Ideas
www.facebook.com/kmartpiemakerrecipes

Kogan Pie Maker Recipes, Hints & Ideas
https://www.facebook.com/
groups/553372021784321/

Top 10 Pie Recipes
https://www.taste.com.au/recipes/collections/
top-10-pie-recipes

65+ of the Best Pie Recipes You'll Ever Bake
https://www.countryliving.com/food-drinks/
g938/best-pie-recipes-0510/

Books & Magazines

McCosker, Kim. **4 Ingredients.** 4 Ingredients.
PO BOX 400. Caloundra Queensland 4551. Australia.

McCosker, Kim. **4 Ingredients Cook 4 A Cure.**
4 Ingredients. PO BOX 400. Caloundra
Queensland 4551. Australia.

McCosker, Kim. **4 Ingredients Chocolate Cakes
& Cute Things.** 4 Ingredients. PO BOX 400.
Caloundra Queensland 4551. Australia.

McCosker, Kim. **4 Ingredients MORE Gluten
Free Lactose Free.** 4 Ingredients. PO BOX 400.
Caloundra Queensland 4551. Australia.

McCosker, Kim. **4 Ingredients The Easiest ONE
POT Cookbook Ever.** 4 Ingredients. PO BOX 400.
Caloundra Queensland 4551. Australia.

McCosker, Kim. **The Easiest Slow Cooker Book
Ever.** 4 Ingredients. PO BOX 400. Caloundra
Queensland 4551. Australia.

Caracciolo, Barbara Elisi. **CRUSTS – The
Ultimate Baker's Book.** Cider Mill Press Book
Publishers LLC. PO BOX 454. 12 Spring Street,
Kennebunkport, Maine 04046.

The Australian Women's Weekly. **The Pie Maker.**
Bauer Media Books, Australia. 2020

Index

CRISPY *on the* OUTSIDE

FRESH & WARM *on the inside*

this is the MAGIC OF PIES